# Forgiveness
# is Green

# Forgiveness is Green

G.F. Sage

QUERENCIA

Querencia Press, LLC
Chicago, Illinois

QUERENCIA PRESS

© Copyright 2022
**G.F. Sage**

LIBRARY OF CONGRESS CATALOGING-IN-PUBLICATION DATA

ISBN 978 1 959110 01 5

www.querenciapress.com

First Published in 2022

**Querencia Press, LLC
Chicago IL**

Printed & Bound in the United States of America

To all the girls like us

and to all the boys that are nothing like him.

# CONTENTS

## *Preface*

This isn't just my story. This is for anyone who has had to live like one of us to survive. The only difference is, I have been blessed with the courage to speak up and write what other survivors have not been capable of speaking about. I cannot speak for every survivor, but I hope by sharing glimpses from my life, and from witnessing the darkest moments of loved ones of mine, I can redefine the stigma that comes with being not only a victim but from sharing our truth.

This is a story in which the beginning feels more like an ending, and all too often in these stories, it is. This is an ode to those who are gone too soon and an ode to the ones who never thought they would make it through. When I started writing the majority of the book that you are now holding in your hands, I was at a very low point in my life. A place of hurting, isolation, abuse, suicidal ideation, and neglect. There were many nights I would lay on the coldness of the floorboards in my room thinking about how no one in my life really knew just how far gone I was. Just how close I had come from making an irreversible mistake. I genuinely never thought that I'd live long enough to have these parts of my life ever be told, and yet here we are. Your gaze through these pages alone is the cause of my divine inspiration. Everything I've lived through led to this moment. Each of the moments before now has meaning because of you.

I hope these pages can inspire you to make a change in redefining what our "normal" should be. To realize the value of rediscovering the person you were before you became the person you had to be. Giving the love and acceptance we often give away to others and instead invest it in ourselves. Getting help, however hard that may be, and finding a safe place that you can call your home. This is not just the start of my story, but the start of so many others. If you choose to at this moment, this could be the start of yours as well.

- G.F. Sage

### Dyke pt. 1

It's junior year and we're sitting in the lunchroom, but I haven't been eating. Instead, I'm trying to digest his disgusting sense of humor or rather, a lack thereof. His hand is on my leg and his eyes are on my lips when he parts his own to release the words that haunt me to this day.

"I could rape the gay out of you," he says.

There is no silence that follows. There is no defense from the group I would have then called friends. This kind of statement raised no red flags; it was nothing out of the ordinary, if anything it was common. I exchange a glance across the table with the girl that I'm seeing, and she's smiling and I'm trying to smile too. Not because I want to, but because I'm expected to, because this is how it is. To appease. To hide our true feelings. To maintain relationships. To not be so sensitive. To pretend, as if our emotions do not belong to us. To act as if we belong to you.

I'm holding back my fangs and when I smile, I show no teeth. Splitting away from the feeling of his hand feeling his way up my thigh. The more it climbs, the more I continue to descend within. Is this the way that I have learned to protect myself, by neglecting myself? I can feel the blood filling inside of my mouth—my blood—from how hard I am biting down. The pressure of this forced gesture is getting the best of me. Compartmentalizing my emotions to avoid the possibility of a commotion, because you know as well as I do how loud girls like us can be. But as loud as we are, we are never loud enough to be heard.

### *Girls like us*

don't talk too much
when men like them tell us not to.

Girls like us fear offending others
and are often too polite for our own good
too afraid to say no
knowing the type of "crazy bitch" it would take to do so.

Girls like us
are told we are too sensitive
too over dramatic
that the scarred skin we cover up
is somehow for show.

Girls like us
don't get better,
we get better at hiding the truth
until moments
come back in movements
from people you thought were friends.

Girls like us
aren't saying all boys are like them
just that the ones that are should be held accountable
and not turned into a role model of what makes them a
man.

### *flinch*

if i flinch
please don't laugh,
because within that involuntary movement
lies a memory i've been trying to forget.

*first published in Sunday Mornings at the River
– Flowers Grow in Graveyards Too*

### *Dissociation*

I sat with legs crossed and eyes closed
as you hit me over and over
and I imagined it wasn't happening to me.

I don't remember why you were enraged.
I don't remember what you were saying.

But I'll never forget your swinging hands meeting my body.
I was just a child.

I pray you never have children of your own.

### Childhood friends

Back in Elementary
you threatened me with a knife
and I couldn't tell anyone
because they might have taken you away,
I grew up afraid to speak up
and you grew up learning how to get away with it.

### The invisible man

"She's a bitch,"
he would say pacing back and forth,
slamming things and throwing things.

    "She's a bitch"
"She's a slut"
    "She's a whore"
"She's a cunt"
    "She's going to hell"

She's this,
She's that,
She's gone.

And though it's been 3 years since they've talked,
she still hears your voice every day.

### It's okay to be angry

When I was younger I would never allow myself to get angry for fear of the correlation found between anger and abuse. Loud noises still startle me to this day, and I never wanted to have to raise my voice to get a message across. I would still get angry, suppressing it not erasing it, as often as I felt it. Pushing it all the way down, until the misplaced emotions would eventually boil over onto myself. Hating and harming myself for not being able to defend myself.

Anger was the demon who lived inside of us. The one that came out with one too many drinks or far too few. Anger was the backhand across my face when I said too much, or when I couldn't speak at all. Anger was the boyfriends of loved ones of mine or the family members we'd point at in the photo albums. It was normalized. It was familiar. It was something I was terrified of and never wanted to be anything like.

We all have moments we are not proud of. But something I continue to remind myself is that truly horrible people do not sit and wonder if they are a bad person or not—they just continue to do bad things unto others. We are all constantly changing and growing, and by not allowing yourself to get angry because you don't want to hurt others you are still hurting someone—yourself. You are not any exception, any less human than anyone else. You are worthy of the same kindness you give away to others. You are allowed to be hurt, to be angry. Your feelings are valid, and without expressing them properly, you will continuously misdirect your anger inwards. There will be times when it's important that we hold the people around us accountable for their actions. By suppressing your emotions you are not only robbing yourself of your own path of growth, but you are also taking away what could be an opportunity for others to gain self-awareness.

When I first started unlearning that anger was inherently a bad thing, I had a hard time managing my own. There was so much that I had been holding onto, that I wanted to spare loved ones of mine from feeling, even if it was a similar hurting that they had inflicted on me. However, when I started to speak up for myself, it would all begin to resurface. Everything I once bottled up would suddenly start to release. I wasn't only mad at you for doing this now, I was mad at you for doing this my whole life. And I'm not just angry for myself, I'm furious for the child whose voice you took away from her. I was and am resentful and overly protective of my inner child.

It goes without saying that allowing myself to have anger, never made me one of the monsters I was afraid of ever being like. Never even close to it. As loud, or as furious as I had become—I might have hurt feelings, but I never made someone afraid of me or what I was going to do to them. I ruined evenings, not lives. I didn't leave bruises, I had arguments—as do most of us. I didn't know how to navigate these feelings I had never allowed myself to have, and it took time trying to figure it out. I'm still figuring it out. Holding myself accountable for my wrongdoings, while allowing myself the ability to stand up for myself.

### Monsters

I learned from you
monsters don't hide under beds,
but in picture frames
and family albums.

***Father***

In the mirror,
I see more of you
than I do of me.
Those eyes are your eyes
and they are crying
because they miss seeing me.

### Silent movie

I remember riding in the back of his car. Behind the driver's seat, with my head in my palm, leaned up against the window. Listening to songs on my fuchsia-colored mp3. The headphone wires were so twisted up and damaged, that you had to hold them wrapped around your fingers at different angles just to hear out of both sides of it. I don't know what they were fighting about this time. I couldn't hear them, or maybe I just wasn't there inside of my body listening. As soon as it started to get loud, I would pull out my mp3 and close my eyes, picturing myself elsewhere.

My mother has had to live the majority of her life with chronic pain. I'd ask her how she was able to maintain her composure while suffering. The feeling like you are covered in fire ants, the bones made of glass shattering together when trying to stand, the burning sensations, and the ongoing throbbing against your already sore and tender limbs. She told me she would picture her pain as if it was attached to a knob. Like turning down the volume of your music, she could picture herself turning down her pain. Detaching herself from what she was feeling. Dissociation is similar in that sense.

"STOP SINGING," He rips the earbud from my ear so quickly and with such force that it hurts.

Everything stops. The music, my singing, my fantasies that I am anywhere else but inside of this vehicle. I return to my body. If dragging nails on a chalkboard could shriek crude words towards you, then it would speak with his mouth. He tells me I have an ugly voice. Only people with beautiful voices should sing.

25

My father tells him that I'm singing because I'm happy, and he asks him to leave me alone. But his hand has already met my knees, and I don't know which crevice of the car's seats my mp3 has landed under due to the impact.

Not only am I not happy, but I am also unaware of the fact that I was singing. Perhaps he was getting louder, and the volume on my music couldn't catch up to him. Perhaps it was a form of self-soothing, singing softly to myself like my mother would when holding me in her arms when I was just a little human. Perhaps it was less of me trying to sing and more of me, however softly, trying to have my voice be heard.

He would call me Mildred, the girl from the book Fahrenheit 451, who had electronic seashells in her ear. Like Mildred, I was also trying to escape with mindless entertainment. Having my earbuds in was a way that I felt like I could maintain what little control I had. I used to blast my music so loud to cover up the screaming that I'm sure I have suffered some form of hearing damage.

It took me a long time and a lot of unlearning to be able to feel comfortable singing again. And though I've learned how to feel comfortable with singing in front of others, I still struggle with feeling comfortable enough in my everyday life to stop myself from dissociating now and then.

I dissociate because you're yelling. Because I'm yelling. Because you're touching me in a way that I'm not comfortable with. Because you're touching me in a way that feels good. Because it's happening all too fast. Because there are too many people in this room. Because I'm sobbing too hard, and my breathing is too sharp. Because I want to tell you to stop. Because I want to tell you no. Because I want to speak up.

I know I have to try to speak up.

### Co-dependent

You said you'd have my back
but when you're gone
I'm spineless without you.

### Unlocked

He's coming,
so you sprint back to the room
which is written with your name on it
but does not belong to you.
Shoving your whole body against the door,
trying to close the damn thing to lock it in time.
That little *clink*
could make or break you
for there is nothing
that can save you
once he's inside.

### The backroads

I used to have conversations with god,
eyes closed,
riding in the backseat,
somewhere along the side streets,
asking him to take me
anywhere other than home.
I became accustomed to a silent plea,
praying that as soon as my eyes would open,
I would be as lifeless as I felt.

  —He, however, never did respond

*"There is a hum"*

There is a hum stuck inside my head
one wishing me dead
and on and on it goes,
and on and on it goes.

*Thin Ice*

You don't realize the value of a breath

    until

      you can't

        come up

          for

              Air.

### Lost in translation

I am
filled
with so
many stories
both written
and unwritten
in a language
you don't
know how to read.

    —you don't understand me

***Re: When you say you love my work***

Does the appreciation stem from the art alone
or more so from the truth inside of it.
Identifying the pain within paintings and
relating it to your own hurting.
For as bare as I have become,
every line represents every inch of me
however, not every line is meant to be read
as not every inch is meant to be seen.
Yet if it was, if I was,
Would you still applaud my creativity?
Would you still glorify me?
Or, would you become horrified by me,
finally seeing me as I always have been?

Both the canvas, and the artist as one.

### *I want to tell you everything*

I would split open my skull if I could
letting every memory spill over and spell out
exactly what had happened and when
but no matter how hard I try to recall those times,
all I seem to remember is that I can't.

### Dyke pt. 2

It's 5th grade and we're sitting in Math class. She's swinging her foot back and forth while taking down notes from the whiteboard. I'm swimming inside of a couple-sizes-too-big, hand-me-down sweatshirt, with my head in my hands. Suddenly her leg swings a little too far and her foot ends up colliding into mine, and for a moment time seems to stop as I look up meeting her eyes.

"Sorry," she mouths, and like that my cheeks turn over to a pastel pink.

I don't respond, not because I don't want to, but because I don't know how to. I don't know how to express these feelings properly because I am unaware of what these feelings are. Instead, I somewhat awkwardly, and yet somewhat lovingly, kick her back. There's a smile on my face that is soon replaced with guilt and shame, for as the bell rings, I know I have to walk the halls alone.

I wasn't surprised to have seen her waiting for me, I was however surprised at how she had decided to greet me. Her leg extended outwards, knocking me off my feet, simultaneously sending the pile of books in my arms to scatter about on the floor. If you suspected this to be the girl from earlier, you have sadly been mistaken. For this was not the girl from my math class greeting me at my locker, but rather the girl from my nightmares. There was nothing accidental about the pain she would inflict upon me.

"You're a lesbian, aren't you?"

That was the first time I have ever heard the word, and though I didn't know what the definition was, I had a good idea that it's meaning was not a good one. I shook my head automatically from side to side, but she wasn't so easily convinced.

"We already know you are; we've heard about you and "

As soon as the name escaped from her lips I could feel a wave of nausea wash over me. ▮▮ was as close to a friend as I had back then. I was new to the school and she was the only one who would allow me to talk to her. She was as close to a friend as I ever had, but she didn't feel like a friend. With her, it felt different. I felt differently.

More strongly. More fondly.

I keep saying it. She was as close to a friend, but she was never a friend. Not to me at least. To the girl at the lockers perhaps, for she saved a chair for her, never a chair for me, and when the girl from the lockers would push me against them, she would stand by and laugh.

It wasn't that I was okay with it, but rather that I understood her, and why she did it. This was what she had to do to blend in, and I preferred it to be me over her. I had never felt this way about anyone before and I knew that I could never feel this way about anyone again. Something was wrong with me. Something so horribly wrong with me that no one could ever be near me. Something I didn't ask for. Something I couldn't control, or hide away, as much as I would try to. And try, I did.

## 1/27/17

I've been broken-in like the spine of a leathery book's backbone.
My teardrops fall from my eyes that mirror my father's
and my smile has been painted on placid
can you not see the cracks at the seams of my composure?

I miss that one girl,
who sat alone at lunch with her nose stuck in a novel,
the same girl who wrote sonnets on napkins
and danced like snoopy to overplayed pop songs.

I haven't seen her in a while,
I haven't found her in the pills,
or in therapy.

Sometimes she walks by, and I chase
her down grabbing her at the ankles,
and she cries so hard until I finally have
to let her go.
I let her go because I love her,
and I just hope eventually she will come back of her own free
will.

### My ending

No one understands how far gone I am these days
how close I've come to my last days
I keep calling out
perhaps I'm not speaking loud enough

Today was supposed to be the day I got better
I told myself I would
I wanted to
I didn't.

I promised myself so long ago
I would live to help someone
But how?
When I cannot help anyone, not even myself.

What am I alive for?
I don't know why I'm alive anymore
I don't have a purpose without being able to save someone
And I know no-one can save me
from myself

### *Moth*

as i walked, i watched my hands turn lilac
i didn't feel the cold,
the street felt closer to the sidewalk,
the headlights felt brighter,
i began to understand how a moth is drawn to the light bulb and
how gnats don't live longer than a week.

***I decided to take my own life***

into my own hands,
and decided the story
I was written into
wasn't on its last page
but on its first page
of a new chapter.

### Death didn't touch you

but you touched me,
hit me,
and used this body as if it were yours.

Death didn't touch you,

but I dress up in all black
and mourn the loss
of the family member
I'll never have.

Death didn't touch you,

and I would never wish it to
but it would have been an easier story for me to tell
because then at least I could talk about you,
I can't talk about you.

Death didn't touch me either,

and you're lucky
because if it had
all these writings would leak,
and all these words
would morph into your name,
I wouldn't be able to protect you anymore.

Unlike you, I don't believe in karma,
but I do believe in guilt
and if death had touched me
then I'm certain that if you could feel anything
at all for me,
It might have touched you as well.

***What I wish I knew sooner***

We don't hate life,
we hate the people around us,
and the situations we are stuck in.

### *This is not how you heal*

They say to forgive is to forget,
so I did.

I forgot what you did to me, and I stayed
stuck in a cycle of forgiving and re-experiencing it all.

Believing it each time, as if it were the first time you told me
it wouldn't happen again.

I didn't become a better person,
I became a broken one.

### *Gaslit*

You became my moral compass guiding me on what's right /
what's wrong / what I'm allowed to feel / what I'm not / telling
me that this is love / when you ask where I am / who I'm with /
who I'm talking to / you just want to protect me / you would
never hurt me / but when you do / it's cause this is what I made
you do / I didn't respond fast enough / I was looking at someone
else the way I should be looking at you / my friends aren't really
my friends / they don't want what's best for us / what's best for
you / it's all because of you / second guessing myself /
wondering if I'm being selfish for even considering myself / I'm
losing myself / we've become so close that I can't make out
where you begin / and where I end / and I end up believing that
this is what I want / I end up believing this was out of love

### This Isn't Love

The walls around you,
were they put in place to protect you,
or to keep you from leaving?

Is this house your home?
Are these people your family?
Is this your life you're living?

You had no choice as to what you would be born into,
So don't let what you can't control
control you.

You have a choice now,
and love is not a condition to stay,
It's a reason to leave in search of it.

### *Your body is your home pt. 1*

The space that your body takes is yours and yours alone.
Anyone else is a visitor
it is not their home,
do not allow them to overstay their welcome.

### *There is strength in walking away*

I used to tell myself, "I don't want him to hit me anymore."
Now I tell myself, "I will never give him the chance to."

### Silence

They say less is more,
which is why I chose my words carefully
until there were no more words for me to use.

Now all this time has passed us by
and I think my silence has said more to you than I ever had.

They say silence is deafening
which I had hoped to be true,
but you were never really one to listen anyway.

### My beginning

No one understands how far ███████████████

██████ I've come ███████████

████████████

perhaps I'm not speaking loud enough

███████████████████████████ I got better

I told myself I would

████████

I did ██

I promised myself so long ago

I would live ████████████

████████

███████████████████████████████████

██████████████

████████████████████████

█████████████████████████████ to save someone

And I ████████████ can save me

from myself

### *A story where she saves herself*

Once I only wished
to be whisked away
by the arms of a beautiful woman.

My princess charming
came a little later than I had hoped
but at least she came.

With time, a beautiful woman had saved me
and I am forever grateful to her,
to myself,
for being the hero that younger me had always hoped I one day
could be.

### *You matter*

You don't need someone to tell you
how you're feeling is valid
but if you think you do
then here I am saying exactly that

***To my best friend's rapist:***

I wouldn't wish you dead because I wouldn't want to grant you that blessing. However, I wish you would die already, that way I know for certain that what happened to her won't happen to anyone else. What you took from her, has taken her years to get back. Blaming herself, hating herself for what happened, while you get to parade around this town like you own it. You don't own shit. Everything in your meaningless life has been handed to you. You're daddy's big little boy following in his footsteps like a fucking lemming, and I can't wait for the day our broken justice system can't protect you anymore and I get to watch you fall from the ledge.

### I don't want to lose control

and wonder where it went,
I want to hand it over freely,
I don't want to have to give in
don't try to convince me.
I waste so much time convincing myself
that this time will be safe
when your touch bares the reminders
of those before you who haven't been.
And you haven't been looking at me quite nearly enough
It's getting harder for me to see you clearly
who you are,
what you are to me,
I need you to look at me,
really look at me.
I need to know you are still here in this moment with me,
that you haven't moved on to the next,
leaving me to myself,
leaving me here with them.

*first published in Sunday Mornings at the River
– Flowers Grow in Graveyards Too

*Rose*

You may feel as small and as insignificant as a pebble,
but let me assure you that you are a seed.

With time and shine
you will show the world just how powerful a seed can be
when you transcend to a beautiful flower.

This is why they call you rose.
Because even in the darkness of the soil
you sprouted,
you grew,
and you rose against it all.

So stay with me my seed,
you have so much potential inside of your very shell.
You are hope,
and although you may be dormant as of now

    —you will grow

### Heroine

From a young age, girls like us are taught that we need saving. Fairytales of being trapped in a tower, or helplessly being carried away by the overpowering villain. We learn we need to endure until our hero arrives and rescues us. But what happens if there is no hero, when there is no one coming to save us?

For me it was denial.

I used to lay awake on my Fisher Price bed with my eyes closed, bringing my hands together, praying that someone would save me. When I was a child, I thought that person would be one of the many adults in my life. As I got older, I thought it might even be the justice system, but for an embarrassingly long time, I had misplaced my hopes of being saved in the idea of being loved by someone else.

There's this saying you might have heard, and if you are anything at all like me you might have even rolled your eyes at it. It's that, "you can't love someone until you love yourself". The truth is you can, but you shouldn't. From my personal experience, not loving myself translated into not caring about how I was treated. Growing up in a dysfunctional household, your definition of what love is and how it should make you feel becomes skewed.

I thought love was who could yell the loudest. The tracking of your whereabouts, and the controlling of what you wear. I thought love was only found in the bottom of empty beer bottles. A side effect, of addiction. I thought it was the accusations and the ritual of apologizing without any wrongdoing. I thought love was the fear of losing them intertwined with the fear of what they might do to themselves if you left. The fear of what they could do to you—again.

Love doesn't leave a bruise and make you buy concealer to cover it up. Love doesn't put a knife under your chin and beg you to stay. Love doesn't throw you down the stairs, breaking your ribs, and breaking you down until you don't know who you are without them.

I would attract, and in some ways welcome, the most toxic situations I had ever been in, because subconsciously, it was ingrained in me that this was not just the love that I deserved, but the only kind of love I knew how to receive. A love that is loveless. An obsession spiraling out of control, with such intensity it burns everything down that tries to come between it.

I never stopped looking for someone to love me, but I decided to become someone that would be healthier to love. Looking at the relationships from those around me, it made me realize I never wanted to be treated like that or treat someone else like that. I started working out because it was a good way for me to expel my suppressed anger. I also wanted to reassure myself that I could not only be strong but feel strong. Especially with my identity of being a lesbian, I knew that I would never have the option to count on a man to protect me. However, as women, or as members of any minority groups, our safety is never guaranteed to us, and I don't know that I will ever feel comfortable in my abilities to defend myself, regardless of how "strong" I can become.

Strength is also more than muscle. It took strength to move out of an unhealthy household. It took strength to push the knife back into my pocket, not into my skin. It took strength to tell my story, to get help, and it takes strength every single day to remind myself that I am more than what has happened to me. It takes strength to admit that I am the person who had these things happen to her. What I'm saying is, the strength you have is not defined by your path of healing. What I'm saying is that just because *you're not healed*, doesn't mean *you aren't strong enough*.

And that little girl, praying to be able to control time long enough to fast forward to the good part lived long enough to have it happen. The hero she'd been expecting never did come, but the one she needed, she became.

### *Reflection*

The hardest apology
is found somewhere between you,
and the image you've been painting of yourself
after all these years.

## *Dyke pt. 3*

"Faggot."

      Says one of the taller boys, as he shoves another student towards one of the workbenches. Colliding into it, he laughs. He has to laugh. I know this, he knows this. Because to laugh is to accept that it's funny to suggest something that is so far from the truth, and to show any other emotion is to declare it to be true.

      I took woodshop because my mother told me this was where the lesbians would be, and as it turned out, I was the lesbian I was looking to find. I was the only girl. I was THE lesbian, the 1 of 1 needed to meet the quota for this outdated stereotype. Although nobody else knew it, for with years of practice, I had become very good at passing. So good, that even though I was out, and I had a girlfriend, I was still subconsciously acting as if I wasn't myself around others.

      My first date that I went on with a girl, I spent the entirety of it convincing myself and acting as if it was not at all a date. I didn't look at her when I wanted to look at her or in the way I wanted to look at her. I didn't touch her, because the concept of closeness with someone I liked, I had learned to be a danger. How quickly the warmth of a stove could be replaced with the shock of the burn in close proximity. I learned how to enjoy others from afar, to enjoy the view, without experiencing it firsthand.

      Self-sabotage was a survival skill I learned, to deny the feelings I had and to act as if I was not experiencing them. Detaching myself from who I was in order to play the role of who I was expected to be. The script handed to me, I had studied over and over as all of us do. I am playing the part of what it means to be a young woman, and he is playing the part of what it means to be the young man. I am expected to date, without having dated too many, to have experience, without having the practice. I am to dress up modestly, and I am to act politely. When I am asked to be his it is not a matter of question, it is supposed to be a matter of instincts. The desire to be with him should have traced back to our need to survive, the rulebook coded into my very DNA. For whatever reason, it wasn't. It was never there.

### *Your body is your home pt. 2*

At time, it might not always feel like a home
in those times it might be wise to redecorate and dust off
the places you have forgotten how to love and appreciate.
There is no shame in rediscovering yourself,
sometimes all it takes is a little fresh paint
to find value in the beauty of your exterior.

## *Makeup*

Your goodness does not reside in your glamor.

Makeup would be nothing but paint,
and paint would be nothing without a canvas such as yourself.

You may claim you are no beauty, yet you are wrong.

As you are a model for beautiful creations highlighting what
was already there prior.

It does not define you but enhance you,
and showcase the beauty you are
with the confidence you radiate
leaving others only in awe.

## *Subjective*

I lack follow-through,
and tend to come across too strongly
regardless of the flavor being
too sweet or too bitter,
I am the cup of coffee that will never quite taste right.
Consistently inconsistent,
and undoubtedly problematic at times.
However, for whatever I lack
I gain self-awareness in
and instead of maintaining stagnant
I will continue to see not what is wrong with me,
but identify the parts of me that still need room to grow,
while appreciating the delicacy in how I bloom.

*"Too much"*

If they call you too much,
perhaps you are too much.
Too open, too honest, and too giving
to someone who does not value all it is you have to offer them.

You'll find someone who does,
but not until you know your worth.

Write down what you bring to the table,
and what you're looking for in return
and don't settle for anything less,
when you have so much to give.

### *This is your home pt. 3*

Do not be fooled into believing that you are unable to handle the
upkeep alone, you do not need someone else to lend a hand
in order to feel at home in your own body.
Have pride in what you have built and created
do not try to stage it for others
for this is a home that is not made to sell,
but to be loved and lived-in by you.

    —Please live in it well

### Loud

Sorry, but
I talk loud
to overcompensate
and make up for all the
times I thought I couldn't speak at all.

### Elm street

This is my normal
shuddering,
heart beating,
twisting between the sheets,
sweaty,
awakened by my own screams.

You always hurt me where I'm most vulnerable
which is why it's no surprise you can find me here too.

### 1,2,3, (Dream sequences)

One...
This is a dream
Two...
he cannot hurt me
Three...
I am safe

One...
I taught myself
Two...
how to change my dreams
Three...
from the age of six 'til the age of twenty-one

One...
I count to three
Two...
to change my dreams
Three...
By blinking once on each count

One...
I talk to myself
Two...
While I'm asleep
Three...
to soothe myself

One...
I am okay
Two...
I am safe
Three...
It is a dream, he cannot hurt me

One...
I wonder how many times

Two...
How many nights
Three...
I will continue to pray myself to wake

One...

How much longer must I count?

Two...

How much more must I take?

Three...

How much more can I possibly have to remember?

Three...

I don't want to remember

Two...

I don't want to have to take it

One...

I don't want to have to count anymore

But I'm afraid of what will happen once I stop. What will happen if I can't wake up. What will happen to me if I realize that these bad dreams are not only bad dreams, but bad memories that I have to live with.

*Authenticity*

I would rather have the courage
to be considered controversial
than settle on being relatable.

How dishonest it is to protect an image of yourself
that doesn't reflect who you are
but how you'd like to be seen.

### *The us vs. them mentality*

Projecting onto others the attributes you don't like about
yourself won't heal the parts of you that are hurting.
It will only further the divide between you and others
adding another reason to back your own bias
that these are the types of people they are
while unaware of the kind you are becoming
by looking at anyone as anything less than human
and yourself as any more than.

*You didn't protect me, so why am I protecting you?*

I leave you nameless in these writings
not wanting others to know
what you did to me
and that it was you
who did it to me.

This isn't out of love
but out of fear.

### Side Effects

I woke up on the floor / watching as the blood trickled down my
head / confusion and fear washing over me / I couldn't stand so
I crawled to the door / pounding on it with my hands hoping
someone would hear me from the other side / I thought I was
dying / screaming out for help / there was so much I didn't
know / how long I've been out / what time it was / or even what
had happened to me / my mom heard me shouting out for her /
but my door had been locked / I wasn't able to reach it so she
had to force it open in order to get to me / and when it did open
her face filled with horror /

*you're bleeding... you're really bleeding...*

and as she helped me up / I threw up all over the floor / it
wasn't until I arrived at the hospital that they informed me that
what happened / was only another side effect / I wish I could
say that this was only the first time / but it was at least the last

### Sarah Quill (seroquel)

I didn't know I needed you until you walked into my life.
You found me where no one else could find me,
in the darkest corners of my mind and you shined the light
and lead the way out for me.
It felt like you saved me, brought out my potential and helped
me better myself.
I was calm when I was with you, I could think clearly,
I expressed myself more freely, I was listened to, and I was
actually heard. I told all my friends about you, about what
we had, and how I didn't know what I would do without
you.

But I did just fine.
I was restless at first, nauseous even,
and it was a hard transition for me when I grew to be
so dependent on you, but I became the light I needed,
and when things got dark again, I didn't beg you to
stay.

I heard the rumors, but I never thought it would actually happen
to me.
I thought we were different.
I trusted you.
Why did you make me better to wind up making me worse?

### *The favorite*

He hates me so much
for being put up on this pedestal,
but he doesn't know how it hurts
to fall off of it.

### *They'd call it an accident*

I used to fantasize
about walking in the middle of the street at night
and getting hit by a car.

That way when someone asked,
"What is wrong with you?"
I would at least have something to show.

### Dysfunctional

I was an angel for what I did.
The cleaning and the pleading,
bartering for the bare minimum,
behaving for the promises of a better tomorrow,
for tomorrow he would change,
along with his words which would finally hold meaning.
Wake up as a new man
as a father, or even as a friend.
I would have settled then for someone that I could trust
instead of someone who I had loved.
Look where love has gone and landed us now,
and remember what trust could have built us instead

    —a relationship, a bond, or even a future together

### *A friend invites me out to a place I haven't been*

I like to be included but I don't like to be persuaded,
small gatherings aren't always a trigger, but
sometimes even one person is one too many for me to handle.

This room is shrinking simultaneously,
as the amount of people are growing increasingly,
my thoughts are racing,
mentally planning out an escape route,
with the chosen excuse lingering on my tongue
words of "I should probably go"
filling the air and changing the tone.

A stranger catches a glimpse of me crying,
now she's asking me what happened
and I know there is no use
for although the pain in wanting to explain will never pass,
neither will the lasting impression I will make If I am honest.

### The misfortune of knowing

(After Elizabeth Todoroska & Breanna Morgan)

It's the way they look at me differently / the awkward pause hanging in the air / and the sound of their throat clearing / when they know / but they don't know what to say / and I feel guilty for telling anyone even when I'm being asked to / even when I want to / the shame settling into sentences from stories you usually only read about / I've lived through them / I know how fictional it sounds / it sounds rehearsed / my nervous laughter sounds sick and it feels wrong when I'm speaking so casually about this but / I'm trying not to damper the mood / I'm trying to make you *not* feel bad for me / I don't need another apology / I just need you to understand / I know you don't see it behind the smile / but I'm trying to make it easier for you to accept me / and if I keep playing it down enough / hopefully you will

## *S.A.D.*

I get lost in the crowd easier than a child does during the
holidays.
My palms become ponds of perspiration and
the meaning to my words becomes lost like a page torn out of a
dictionary.

I'm not okay, but I'm telling you I am.
I want to be a part of your normal,
and perhaps I would have been if
it wasn't for what had happened.

I can still be sociable, I don't have to be shy for you to try to
understand that my disorder is more than a trend you can
cling to in order to seem more relatable and quirky when you
are insecure about yourself.

Social anxiety stems from trauma during childhood,
and it can stay with you until the end of your life.

You don't wake up with it.
You don't ask for it.
You don't want it.
And you will never know how it feels to be seen as less than,
when you have been through more than anyone else could
imagine.

I know I'm not weak, but I feel weak,
and as the night is young—I feel young,
lost in a sea full of strangers,
longing to finally be found as I am, as I choose to be,
not for what I had no say in, and what I lack control of.

### On my beautiful woman in a spy movie shit

I blame myself for my actions,

even when it is in reaction.

Keeping apologies on me like a pack of tissues,

ready to pull out and be used

with my voice soft, and my eyes low.

My laugh is not only made of habit, but also as a welcome

to a series of unsolicited remarks.

My laugh is lost in translation for it is not made from joy, but of
nerves along with my apologies that are not genuine,

but fear driven,

as is my submission in general.

Where I may submit to survive,

I will also kill to live.

And while you are distracted,

I am planning.

*We are the stories we tell ourselves*

What you envision is of fiction
a false dictation of the mind
repeating lines after lines,
convincing you each time
that you are not good enough,
and without challenging these thoughts
you will become these thoughts
letting your stream of consciousness overflow
into your reality.
A self-fulfilling prophecy which could be of benefit
if you change what you manifest from what you fear,
to what you dream.

*Stop on this page*

Read me aloud:

My voice however how loud or how soft deserves to be heard.
My body's reflection is not a representation of it's worth.
My needs are not to be compromised by another's wants.

I am strong for I have made it this far.
I am deserving of being loved in the way that I love others.
I am able to achieve what I desire.

I am enough.
I am beautiful.
I am worth it.

*Passive*

I still don't know how
to say no without a
thank you attached.

### *"I know you feel like you were abused"*

I don't "feel like" / I was. / What I feel like, is what you like to
call, "playing devil's advocate" / as disbelieving victims of
violence and making yourself feel less ashamed for siding with
their abuser / I don't know how many times I have to go over it
again / why must I go over the most horrific moments in my life
for your amusement / again and again, to convince you / It's not
my job to convince you / from my experience / it hurts more
when it's someone you love not believing you / for a long time I
didn't believe myself / maybe it wasn't that bad / maybe even
with my mouth stitched shut or my tongue cut out from inside
me, I had still asked for it / you watch me make myself sicker to
try to make you understand / rapid shallow breathing and
throwing up on the bathroom floor / carving myself open with
my fingernails and pulling out clumps of hair / I could
completely break down in front of you, beyond repair /
confiding in you / and still leave you feeling nothing / nothing /
like a news coverage of a mass shooting / it doesn't affect you
until it happens to you / and I pray it never does

### I wasn't lying

What hurt me more than him
was you not believing me
when I told you what happened.

***"I had no idea!"***

You knew the signs,
but when you saw them
you pretended they were never there.
You were too good to be real to someone else,
not wanting to dirty your hands with the knowledge
that I am not okay or that you could lose me to myself.

Now that the signs have been taken down,
now that I am okay,
you like to pretend that you never knew
what was happening and you like to tell everyone
if only you had known and what you would have done.
but I know what you've done.

Nothing...

    —Is that really how you felt?

### *Opening up*

The problem isn't with opening up
but to who & how soon.

You won't know if it was a mistake,
but if it was, that fault is not your own
for I don't know what could be wrong enough in a person
to have someone confide in you just to later use it against them.
Regardless of what someone could say about you,
it will always say more about them
and I would rather know what kind of person they really are.

*Dyke pt. 4*

Instead of following my own instincts, I had learned how to hide them, quietly and inconspicuously. I was never made for Broadway, and it didn't take long for others to take notice of me. Conversations with my mother had led me to see a therapist, and though she had meant to help I had never felt more confused.

Her leg swings over, in one hand a pen and in the other a clipboard. "Why don't you just be gay," my therapist asks. "Fly your freak flag at school, and not care what anyone else thinks?"

"I don't know if I'm gay," I respond with my eyes towards the floor and my hands shaking in my lap.

"But you don't like boys?"
"I don't think I do, no."
"And you think you like girls?"
"Yes," My voice breaks as I respond.
"Then you're gay."

She says it matter-of-factly, tossing up the hand holding the pen.

"I don't want to be gay."

"But you are," I can hear the annoyance in her voice, the spite of my denial showing up between the shortening of her sentences.

"But I don't want to be gay."

This conversation was not one that my mother, nor my therapist, or perhaps many others had understood at the time. My therapist could not wrap her head around the concept of why someone would rather live their life as a lie than to live out their truth. What she didn't know was that sometimes the lie you get so used to telling others feels more like a home than the truth you don't let anyone else know. The truth felt more like isolation, the very representation of a target on my back, the target that I would have to paint myself and declare where it was loudly enough for all the others to know where to take aim. I was pressured into painting it without first preparing for how I would protect myself when the arrows would fly.

I came out before I was ready to come out, and it didn't feel like I got to come out of the closet; it felt like I was pushed out of it. But make no mistake, I know I was one of the lucky ones. I lost friends, but I didn't lose my home. I lost opportunities, but I didn't lose my family. I lost the feeling of any remaining normalcy that I was so desperately trying to cling to, but I didn't lose my life as a result of being who I am. I was granted a blessing that not all of us are given. Which is why it is never up to any therapist, family member, friend, or partner to decide when it is your time to come out. I wasn't prepared, but I got lucky, not all are as privileged as I was.

When you are ready, know that you are not alone. That you were never alone. That there are so many of us like you that will accept you for who you are, for who you like or don't like, and we will never ask you to be anyone other than yourself. Instead, we will share drinks, as well as stories, gathering around each other lighting an emotional bonfire. Setting ablaze the painful memories with our laughter, one at a time, knowing it might not be any easier, but we will continue to grow stronger. This is the house that is always a home, needing no invitations, or directions. To find your way here there is a map within yourself, and no matter how long the journey to get here will take you, know that I'll be waiting for your arrival along with the others. You are loved, and you are accepted, as you are, and as you will be. I believe in you, as do so many others, because all of us at one point had to be you, and I can't wait for the day that you can comfortably be one of us.

### *On beliefs*

I find it more valuable to befriend many with views other than
my own than to limit myself from the opportunity to grow
by missing out on the importance found in the dialogue between
what is known and what is a matter of interpretation.

### One with melancholy

I don't see myself as the woman I am today
I see the girl I used to be.

For as much as I have grown,
I am small.

Rather, I feel small when I am vulnerable
and I am vulnerable as often as I am healing,
retelling and reliving.
I'm hanging in between two realities
trying to find who I am inside of who I had to be.
It's hard to see yourself as anything other than what's been done
to you.

My reflection is made from a collection of all the times
I didn't say no, even when I wanted to,
and I shame myself for not being able to.

I feel small,
for I am afraid,
that as strong as I have become,
I will never be strong enough to protect myself,
and that fear is not only mine but of many survivors,
and I know this is the part where I am supposed to reassure
you, and comfort you,
to say that you are not alone,
but where that would usually bring comfort,
it brings me to tears.

### We treat our girls like trees

A tree that falls in the forest makes a sound,
as does the girl who screams no.
Just because no one was around to hear it,
does not mean she didn't make a sound.

*first published in Celestite Poetry – Issue 1*

*To lie*

Lying isn't nearly as hard as you would think it is
when you've been doing it for as long as I have been,
protecting him from the consequences,
and myself from the truth.

Lying isn't nearly as hard as you would think it is
when "I love you's" aren't made from love,
but from habit and fear of what would happen if we didn't say it
back.

Lying isn't nearly as hard as you would think it is
when it's more socially acceptable to disregard our own feelings
in an effort to spare a stranger from the awareness
that we are human and that sometimes we are not okay.

Lying isn't nearly as hard as you think it is
when the truth is often dismissed and disbelieved
leaving victims like us ashamed for speaking up
while our abusers feel proud
continuously able to act out
without repercussions.

Lying isn't nearly as hard as you think it is
when the truth doesn't set us free
as we are told it will,
but isolates us.

*Prey*

I am not defenseless,
I am harmless
that is a difference you
do not know.

***To the boys that are nothing like him***

You are the boys that I would want my daughter to meet, dripping with confidence, without a drop of arrogance underneath. Sweet without the reason to be, drumming to your own beat with kindness in your eyes. You are emotionally available, and you can communicate with your words without having to show your fists. Reliable and able to hold others accountable, you have a mind of your own and any boy like you will always have a friend like me to root you on, for though at times you may feel as rare as you are, you are the embodiment of the change that we could all benefit from.

*Family*

We call our family members by the same names, but they are not always the same to us as they are to you, and sometimes, they are not our family at all.

*Overshadow*

When I was in the dark I would call your name, stretching my arms out trying to search for yours. I didn't know what was happening to me, where I was, who I was, but I held onto the hope that you would find me and take me away from this horrid unknown. I found the light switch located inside of a question I didn't expect you to answer with honesty, even when I had asked you to. And when the lights came on, and I saw you as you were, I realized you were not at all the person I was looking to find. For you knew. You always knew. You knew where I was, and what was happening to me, but you kept me in the dark. You didn't lay a hand on me, but it was by your hands. Your hands alone that allowed it to happen. You kept me there, for all those years, knowing I was being abused, and knowing that this was not a safe place to come back to, but still you called it our home. Your desire of being wanted mattered more to you than my need to be safe, and I cannot forgive you for what you've done, but now at least I know just what you did.

***Outlines***

I wonder why it is that I often shy away from others,
denying the possibilities of friendships found within strangers.

Until I remember, as I always do,
when the outline of someone else
fills into the shape of someone like you.

### *Hope is in the children*

I come from a long line of hurt and broken homes made from
broken people passing the buck onto their children
instead of trying to better themselves.

This family tradition changed with my mother and will finally
end with me personally.

I will not willingly bring life into this world until I can find love
and light within myself. I will not hope for the best for my
children. Instead, I will give them the best that I can give them,
and I will love them the way they were meant to be loved—
without expectations and unconditionally.

### 10 Years

10 years ago I daydreamed of dying
in the back of a car I couldn't drive,
I felt like cargo always being transported around from here to
there, never having a say of where I wanted to be.

10 years later I daydream of living a life with meaning
in the front of a car that I bought myself,
I feel like I always have a choice
of where I want to be.

10 years from now
It won't matter where I go,
as long as I am as free
and as proud
as I am today.

### When do we finally grow up?

Is it,

When the rain no longer means rain boots but back pain?

When you make the switch from using both feet to touch the pedals to just the one while playing racing games at the arcade?

When we rewatch our favorite childhood movies and finally laugh at the jokes we didn't understand back then?

For me it's,

When I'm looking at you as more than a hero, but a human, the one who raised me, seeing you for all that you are and appreciating you for all that you've done. Knowing you for who you are, more than who you are to me.

When I'm able to see myself as I am. No longer letting the weight of my decisions be determined by the weight of the disappointment from the people around me. To be able to accept myself even when I feel as if I am acting as someone else entirely, knowing that even my poor decisions are still my decisions. That this too, is me.

When I am capable of having that much needed compassion for others. To be vulnerable and open with myself and to be willing to have the patience to offer my understanding to those with views differing from my own. To know when it is a time to educate, when it is a time to listen, and ultimately, when it is time to respect my own growth by letting that person go.

***To someone like me:***

They say leaving is the hardest part, and it was. I don't know how I got free from him, but all that matters is that I did. I've always hoped that if somewhere there was someone like me stuck in a similar situation, that they were rooting for me to make it out as much as I would have hoped that they would too. This idea of mine, of living for more than me but for someone like me, has kept me from making an irreversible mistake.

I used to really hate myself. I thought no matter how badly it hurt, that somehow, I deserved it. I told myself I was a burden to others and that I didn't deserve to live. But if there is anything at all that you can learn from me and my story, let it be this—I was wrong. I was so, fucking wrong. We are the stories we tell ourselves, and the story I had been telling myself for so long was a lie. I wasn't born hating myself. I learned how to from others. I spent so much time asking what was wrong with me that I could never realize what was actually wrong with them.

I didn't hate myself. Not really. What I hated was this version of myself that I became in order to keep the peace and survive. I wasn't "too nice" as everyone would say I was—I was too scared. I wouldn't set boundaries, and I feared upsetting others because I was afraid of how they would react. Subconsciously, I associated anger with abuse, and I would do anything to avoid reliving my trauma.

I thought the only way out for me was in death, but what I didn't know was that I didn't have to kill myself to put an end to this life of mine. Instead, I got help. And I'm not going to lie to you—it was embarrassing for me. Sharing my story made me feel insecure, and leaving my abuser was the most terrifying experience I have ever faced. I felt like I was lying even when I was telling the truth because people around me had a hard time believing how someone as seemingly bubbly as myself could have experienced such a traumatic upbringing. I didn't fit into their archetype of what a victim of abuse was, and many of us don't, because we are not only victims, we are survivors. They don't see us as we are, and so we learn to see ourselves as less than. But we are so much more than any of the words I could possibly string together to describe the ongoing struggles we've endured. We have made it this far. You have made it this far.

I know I can't convince you that it's not your fault, because at the time no one could convince me that it wasn't my fault either. But if you could picture someone else going through exactly what you're going through right now, and if you know that they don't deserve it, then you are no exception. If you can't live for you, then live for someone like you—someone like me. Become the person you've always dreamed you could be and be the voice for others like us. Show the world that we are not another sad story that needs saving. Today, you could save a life—you've already saved mine. Be the reason I had to live and I promise to always be yours.

Sincerely,
this is your sign.

***Step by step***

Ask yourself,
what can I do today for a better tomorrow?

*7/9/22*

I am not healed / I am bandaged / I haven't stopped the bleeding
underneath / I've stopped the spreading / you would not believe
how the sound of a laugh / could send me into a spiral / how the
mention of him / depletes the air from my lungs / how I'm telling
you it gets better / it does / but I can't tell you when it's over / I
don't know that it's ever over / where this book ends my story is
still being written / I am still becoming / still replaying / reliving
the moments I've misplaced in my mind / it's like making sense
of objects in a dark room / like inkblot's on paper / or jigsaw
pieces clicking together / I may not find all the pieces / I might
never be whole / I may not always be living / but I am alive /

I am alive

*Abby*

Having the privilege to watch you bloom beautifully
into the person, you were always meant to be
inspires me to do the same.

I can't wait for the world to finally meet you and see you
for who you are.

### *Speak up*

Speak up
and if your voice
has been silenced,
allow me to turn mine
up a notch.

## Deja Vu

It didn't end with you—it started with you,
you set the standard of what normal was for me.
I never thought twice about people that reminded me of you
I let them treat me the way you would
It didn't matter who they were to me
Someone I hardly knew or someone I've known for years,
a coworker, a boss, an acquaintance, or a friend
it never mattered.

People like you can be anyone,
or be anywhere,
and they already are.

It doesn't matter how many times
I have to meet you again,
or how hard it will be to leave,
all that matters is that I will.

   —I always will.

### *Forgiveness is green*

Forgiveness is the growth in my mother's eyes,
green with flecks of sunshine
as if nature is speaking through her.
I can't help but wonder how nature feels
about privacy and personal space.
Perhaps It's indifferent like she is,
forgiving us for taking it for granted
hoping we'll actually change.

I want to change,
I want to forgive you.

But if forgiving you means giving into you
then I won't.
I won't have closure
I'll have boundaries
and unlike nature
I'll grow into my own.

## Under the sun

I thought I saw you standing under the sun the other day. Your worn-out jeans, and your graying hair. I thought I caught you looking my way, so I covered my face with my coat. It's funny, isn't it? Unknowingly hiding behind the same coat you had bought me all those years ago. Do you remember when one of the buttons fell off and you offered to zip tie it back on for me? I don't know if I laughed then, but I'm crying now.

You had the potential to be the man I wanted you to be, the man I needed you to be. You could have been everything, and it wouldn't have taken much. I wish when I had asked for space, you had given me space. I wish when I asked to not come back to your house, you wouldn't have forced me. I wish when I grabbed the sides of mom's car with my fingers, that you hadn't grabbed me by my ankles. I wish you didn't buy me all those things I wanted when none of it was ever what wanted. It's horrible, isn't it? I wish there was a better way for me to say it, but I can't just keep wishing, can I?

I want to tell you that you were right, I actually do enjoy the freedom found within the open roads. It's nice to feel like you have somewhere you're headed to when you have nowhere to go. I know that's something we both can relate to. Strange how similar we can be, especially when we both are longing for the same thing, yet something so entirely different, as we both are missing me.

Standing in the sand, I'm not sure, even with my face in front of yours, that you would notice me. I am no longer someone you could recognize, and I am proud of that. The invisible baggage I've carried no longer results in a slouch, and for all the tears I've cried, nothing can drown out my smile. Death is no longer a craving of mine or a solution. I've found life to be more satisfactory when you have the freedom to live for yourself. I know you don't get it, do you? I cannot live for you, I could never have lived for you. I tried to for more than half of my life, and if I had continued to do so, I would have died as a result.

I don't think you are the man on the beach. But I like to believe it could have been you. That the two of us could be able to enjoy the same view together without having to be together at all. Because I don't want to reconcile or try to make amends. I just want us to both be able to live for ourselves and to take joy in the little pleasures that life has to offer. That one day you may find the light you admire inside of me, inside of yourself.

*Emerald*

You are not obligated to forgive anyone.
There is more than one way to accept what happened to you,
and you are not going to heal going back to what will keep
hurting you.

That's not to say there aren't those that can change,
but it is to say the opposite is also true.

You won't know which it will be,
and it's not up to anyone else to decide for you.

### *Get free, sage*

Growing up I had this pen pal named Martin who lived in Sweden. We met through a popular MMO RPG, and what started out as casual conversations while playing stemmed into a beautiful friendship. At that time, I had moved to a new area and could never quite fit in well enough to befriend anyone, but I had Martin and he made me feel less alone.

We always talked about music, recommending different artists and albums for each other to listen to. I'll never forget this one song he chose for me. The track was titled, "Get Free" and it was nothing like I had ever heard. At first, I was put off by just how different it was, but after him insisting that I should keep listening to it, I eventually grew to love it as much as he did, if not more.

I don't know if Martin knew what was happening in my family or how badly I needed someone to write to, but he always knew something was wrong. I didn't have to tell him. He just knew. That song became more than a song but a deeper understanding between the two of us. Whenever we would talk, and I would seem distressed he would remind me that I could still Get Free just like the song said, that I would get through this.

A decade has passed, and I am free, and though I wish it would have happened a lot sooner, I am forever grateful for him encouraging me to keep holding on. I always told him I wanted to be a writer and that if I ever wrote a book I would dedicate some part of it to him, and so this is his part. Thank you, Martin, for seeing the potential in me and for seeking the kindness inside of yourself to understand me without ever having to ask what was wrong with me. Your words became my religion and your friendship influenced me to grow beautifully into my own. I aspire to be the kind of person you were to me to someone else out there.

Perhaps I'm already like Martin. I don't know what's happening in your life as you read this, and I may not know you at all. But I know how you are feeling matters. I may not have all the right words to say, but I do have two. Get free. I know you will get free, because you are stronger than you believe and you will find a way out. You are not alone. You are never alone.

And if one day you too find someone looking for a reason, just one reason to stay a little longer—give them a reason, or better yet, a song. For with time, words tend to be forgotten, but everyone always remembers the lyrics to their favorite song. So, make it a good one, something they've never heard before, and if they don't like it at first, ask them to listen again. It'll help buy them the time they need until they can find a way to free themselves.

### *Thank you*

You have now officially made it to the end, and lucky for you I have saved the best for last. This page is a special thank you to the beautiful souls and minds that have helped whether directly or indirectly make this book possible.

Firstly, if it wasn't for the endless support and love from my mother, I wouldn't have had the courage to express myself as openly as I have in my writings. I wouldn't have had the courage to share my words with anyone. She's always been my biggest fan and the biggest believer in me since the very beginning. I remember all the days racing home to her after school so I could practice my lines with her for slam. I remember all the night's she stayed up with me after a long shift to give me advice on one of my pieces. I remember all the times I told her I couldn't, and I also remember all the times she made me believe that I can. I am so proud to say for the both of us that I finally did it. Mom, I love you and I thank you for setting the foundation for me to become the beautiful woman I have grown to be.

Next, I would like to thank my best friend of 9 years, and the ketchup for my mustard. Amanda, I know you haven't ever been really into the poetry scene, but you have always been there to help me when I needed someone to bounce ideas off. You are brutally honest when it is most needed, and continuously push me to better myself. Thank you for all these years of supporting me and thank you for being one of the strong women I could write about.

I would also like to thank three very talented writer friends of mine, Elizabeth, Lois, and Kristen. Elizabeth, I met you only a few years ago but it feels like I've known you for much,

much longer. You are one of the most driven and talented minds I have met, and your writing continues to inspire me to achieve more with my own. You have given me so many hours of late-night advice that I could never repay you, and I'm always so excited to see what's next for you.

Lois, thank you for supporting me after all this time. Your voice memos and long text messages of wisdom over the years really have meant the world to me. Thank you for all the laughs we've shared, and for encouraging me that I could do this.

To Kristen, I don't know if I've ever told you how much I look up to you. We both have a burning passion for writing and while I've tended to take more of the beaten path, you've had the persistence and confidence to take the more traditional approach with your schooling. After writing a lot of these pieces, I would smile to myself, eager like a child to share with you what I had written. Your praise and support has helped me to bloom. Thank you for acknowledging the potential inside of me before I could understand what it was. And an additional thank you for helping me piece together the blurb for this very book!

Another very important person to me in my life is my wonderful girlfriend, Colleen. She has been the sunshine beaming down on me throughout my darkest of days, and the reason I finally hit that submit button to Querencia Press. It was 4am when I woke up from being dead asleep and read the email of acceptance on my phone. We sat up for hours the both of us smiling and covered in tears realizing that the dream is finally a reality. That will continue to be the proudest moment of my life.

On that special note, thank you to Emily and Savannah, the incredible people behind Querencia for taking a chance on me and giving hope to the family members and friends surrounding me. I don't believe my words could have found a better home than with the two of you and for that I cannot thank you enough.

Lastly, I would like to thank the reader for making it this far and for purchasing this book. I hope to use the proceeds I make to prove that not only my dreams can come true, but that anyone's can as long as you are determined enough, and that it is never too late. My mom grew up poor, born into a bad family dynamic, and has fought in so many ways her whole life to just survive. She has always wanted to visit Italy, but she has never had the means to be able to. I remember one day we were out on a walk together and she told me that she finally accepted that it was too late for her and it never would happen. It was at that moment I knew what I wanted more than anything else in this world, and that was to prove her wrong in the best way possible. So thank you reader, for not only making my dream come true but for helping me try to make hers come to fruition as well. If you can learn anything at all from this book, let it be that it is never too late to create the life you deserve.